W9-AHB-935

The Weed
With An Ill Name

Originally Published in the 1800's
by The American Tract Society

Grace & Truth Books
Sand Springs, Oklahoma

ISBN # 1-58339-055-3
Originally published in the 19th century
Current printing, Grace & Truth Books, 2004

All rights reserved, with the exception of brief quotations.
For consent to reproduce these materials, please contact the
publisher.

Cover design by Ben Gundersen
Artwork by Randy Read

Grace & Truth Books
3406 Summit Boulevard
Sand Springs, Oklahoma 74063
Phone: 918 245 1500

www.graceandtruthbooks.com

Table of Contents

The Elms

Chapter 1

A LETTER

Several letters arrived at "The Elms" one autumn morning. One of them was for Mrs. Gray. It read:

My Dear Sister and Brother,

Thank you very much for your kind offer to take care of George and Fanny while we are away. We gratefully accept. It will be an overwhelming comfort to know that our dear children are safe and well cared for while we are so far away.

However, it is only fair to tell you that we fear your nephew and niece might not behave as well as you expect them to. It is not easy for parents to talk about their children's imperfections. We know that both George and Fanny have many good qualities. They are honest, loving and usually obedient. We think they are intelligent for their age.

I am sorry to add that Fanny sometimes loses her temper. The slightest misunderstanding easily offends her. I'm afraid her brother tends to be proud and arrogant, especially towards those whom he thinks are inferior to him. This has definitely caused us quite a few problems. I am afraid that these bad tendencies will give you some trouble. Yet ...

"Temper and pride," said Mr. Gray seriously, after he and his wife had read this part of the letter. "We shall have a serious matter on our hands."

"On our hearts, too," added Mrs. Gray.

"I suppose so, Rachel. It will be on our hearts, too," said her husband.

"Perhaps my sister has exaggerated her children's faults," Rachel suggested hopefully.

"That's not very likely," replied Mr. Gray. "Parents don't usually do that. Besides, both temper and pride are so common in human hearts. It shouldn't surprise us to find them there. We don't need to cross the bridge before we come to it, Rachel. We will find out soon enough what these children are really like. The first thing we must think about is your journey to London. When do you plan to go?"

"Well, sister Martha is going to set sail early next week. I had better leave the day after tomorrow," said Mrs. Gray.

"Why don't you go tomorrow, Rachel? You and your sister will have a lot to talk about. It will be a long time before you see each other again."

"Perhaps we will never see one another again, James," said Mrs. Gray with a sigh and a tear.

"I hope you will, my dear," answered the husband. "Let's hope that a few months in a warmer climate will restore Mr. Franklin's health."

Now, without continuing this conversation any further, it might be a good idea to explain who the speakers were and what they were talking about.

Mr. Gray was a wealthy farmer. He had a large farm and lived in a beautiful house. He had a reputation for being an excellent employer, and he was well educated. Though he did not socialize much or have a lot of friends, those who knew him respected him very much. Mrs. Gray was a kind, gentle, and intelligent lady. She was also well-respected. Like her husband, she delighted in doing good things for everyone around her.

Mr. and Mrs. Gray were happy because they made themselves useful. They served others the way all Christians should, but they also had their trials. God tries the faith and patience of those who love Him in many different ways. We can be sure that when He does this, it is for their benefit, "That they may be partakers of his holiness," Hebrews 12:10. When they are in trouble, their heavenly Father has compassion on them and gives the strength to bear their heaviest burdens. He comforts their souls so they can say, "It is good for us that we have been afflicted," Psalm 119:71.

Mr. and Mrs. Gray's sorrows and troubles had nothing to do with money. The farmer had never had any large losses in his business. He was a prosperous man, and neither he nor his wife wanted any more wealth than they already had. They believed that great wealth led to great temptations. They wanted to put what they already owned to good use. They used it to serve God and help their fellow man rather than trying to get more.

There are other sorrows in life besides those that have to do with poverty and money losses. The Grays had experienced them. They lost several children. Two of them died while they were only babies, and another little girl died when she was five years old. One beloved son was their comfort and hope. At fifteen years old, his life was suddenly ended by a sad accident. Now the farmer and his wife were middle aged. Not one of their sons or daughters was still alive.

You reader, can you imagine how very sad they must have been? They did not criticize God. During all these losses, He helped them submit to His sovereign will. They could say as Job did when his children all died, "The Lord gave, and the Lord hath taken away; blessed be the name of the Lord," Job 1:21.

Some people wondered how Mr. and Mrs. Gray could be so happy after they had suffered so much. The reason for their peace and joy was really no secret. It had been very hard for them to lose every one of their children. They believed in God's wisdom and kindness. When they cast their burdens upon Him, He gave them strength, and gave them victory over sorrow through the Lord Jesus Christ. "Cast thy burden upon the Lord, and he shall sustain thee: he shall never suffer the righteous to be moved," Psalm 55:22.

Now another trouble had come, and it was threatening them like a dark, distant cloud. Mrs. Gray had a very dear sister, Martha, who was a lot younger than she. This sister lived in London. Her name was Mrs. Franklin. Her husband was wealthier than the Gray's, but he had been terribly sick for a long time. The doctors were afraid that he would never recover. They said that there was nothing more they could do to help him. If he traveled abroad and visited a country with a warmer climate than England's, his health and strength might come back.

The Franklins quickly packed their bags and prepared to travel. It wasn't a good idea for the children to go with their parents. So the Grays kindly and willingly offered to take care of them.

Since I have explained all this, the reader should now be able to understand the letter at the beginning of this chapter. The reader should also understand a little bit of conversation which followed. Arrangements were being made for Mrs. Gray to leave home the next morning to say goodbye to her sister. The next week, when she came home, she was going to bring her nephew and niece, George and Fanny Franklin, with her.

Because it is a rainy day, I can't go out to play in the fields.

Chapter 2

TWO MORE LETTERS

Children's trials usually are not so deeply seated as those of older people. They are also more willing to accept hopeful ideas and to enjoy the present. George and Fanny shed many tears as they parted from their parents. They almost certainly hoped for a happy meeting again when their dear father would be healthy and strong.

In the meantime, they excitedly looked forward to visiting their uncle and aunt in the countryside. It is not surprising that after only a few days had gone by, they began to enjoy their life at The Elms, though in many ways, the farm was quite different from their own home.

Their loving and wise relatives did every thoughtful and reasonable thing they could think of to make them happy. Maybe the best way to prove this is by showing two letters very nearly as they were written. George and Fanny wrote these, without any help from their aunt and uncle, to their parents a week or two after they arrived at The Elms. This first letter is from George Franklin, who was about eleven years old.

Then we got into a railroad car which was clean and nice.

My Dear Father and Mother,

I promised to write you soon. I am going to do it now, because it is a very rainy day. I can't go out to play in the fields. The day after you went on board ship, we had a very good train ride from London. Everything was already packed and ready to go, you know. We just had to have our trunks and bags sent to the station. We followed behind them in a taxi. The taxi was very dirty, and it was all Robert's fault. He could have chosen a better one if he had wanted to. I think he did it to tease me. I did not care.

Then we got into a railroad car which was very clean and nice. When we reached the Westshire Station, Uncle James was waiting for us with his buggy and a strong horse. Did you know that The Elms is more than five miles from Westshire?

It was not a plain old buggy. It was a gentleman's buggy. It was nice enough for anybody to ride in, so I didn't mind. Of course, Uncle James does have a carriage. It is rather old fashioned and made for the country. He had to take the buggy because we had so much luggage.

I haven't seen Uncle James for so many years. He says it has been five or six years since he was in London. I wouldn't have recognized him if Aunt Rachel hadn't pointed him out. She looked out the window when the train stopped and said, "Fanny and George, there is your uncle." Then I looked out too. I saw a tall person who was wearing a dull, old coat and a straw hat. Even so, I like Uncle James a lot. He is very, very good to me. He has even given me a pony to ride almost every day. I got a straw hat like his now, and it is so comfortable. I wear it out in the harvest fields and when I am riding

I have a nice room and so does Fanny. They have pretty beds and dressers. Of course, they aren't as nice as our rooms at home. We shouldn't expect that since this is such an old farm house.

Aunt Rachel is really very kind. We all eat and read together in the parlor. There are three maids, but there aren't any man-servants. They only have a man who works in the yard and garden. His name is Sam. He cleans tools, the barn, and other things. He does not help serve our meals, and I am glad. He is not fit at all to come near anybody. Our Robert is much cleaner. Besides him, there are four farm servants who sleep in the house. They all have breakfast, dinner and supper in a large hallway. Of course, we don't have anything to do with them. I go out into the harvest fields with Uncle James. He is very busy now, I mean his men are, cutting down corn. Uncle James expects harvest to be over in about a month.

A teacher is going to come three times a week from Westshire to give me lessons. I don't know what kind of a man he is. I haven't seen him yet. Aunt Rachel is going to teach Fanny. I guess you know all about that.

I can't think of anything else to say. I hope Father will get well soon. I wish I were with you. It would be so much fun to be on a ship and I would like to see different countries. I think I will be very happy here until you come home again. I'm going to like it better here than being at school anyway.

Your loving son,
GEORGE FRANKLIN

P.S. Aunt Rachel is going to write to you and Fanny already wrote. I don't have any messages to put in from them.

Letters often reveal more of their writers' true character than the writers would like. The above letter does not exactly show George Franklin's good side. Some of his selfishness and arrogance, as well as a little pride, are there for everyone to see. It sticks out in the very first sentence when he says he did not write to his parents in order to make them happy. He wrote because there was nothing better to do on that rainy day.

Every part of the letter proves how much he was only thinking of himself and what he enjoyed. How little he thinks of any other person shows. He is so concerned about how people dress and look. Even when he mentions his father and his illness, he does not seem to care very much. He doesn't even ask how his mother is getting along.

It is true that he writes some thoughtful, kind things about his uncle and aunt. This is because they give him what he likes. It is easy to imagine that he already half despises them for not being as rich as his own parents and for not showing off what they do have. The way he speaks about his future teacher and his uncle's servants proves that his mother was right. She said he was proud and arrogant towards those he thinks are beneath him.

We will not be too hard on George Franklin. He did have kinder feelings in his heart than he showed with his pen. Now let's read Fanny's letter. It is shorter than her brother's.

My Dearest Mamma,

I am so glad I can finally write to you and tell you how much I love you and dear, dear Papa. It makes me so sad when I think about how sick he is and how worried it makes you. I hope I won't upset you when I tell you that I cry myself to sleep almost every night. I think about you both all the time. I wish I could see you. I want to hug you again and again and tell you how much I love you and how sorry I am. I hope I never did anything to upset you or make you sad.

Oh, Mamma, please make Papa get well as soon as you possibly can. I will be so glad when you come home and when Papa is as strong as he used to be.

Please, Mamma, don't think that I am not happy. I am as happy as I could possibly be away from home and you. Aunt and Uncle are so kind and good. I like her for a teacher much better than I did Miss Giles. She explains everything so nicely. It's because she really understands the lessons. You didn't think Miss Giles did, remember? We also take such nice walks together. We have gone out and picked blackberries two or three times.

Uncle James is such a godly man. He reads the Bible and prays every morning and evening in the servants' hall. There are three servants. One is a house maid, one is a cook. The other one helps milk the cows. I'm so excited, Mamma, because Aunt Rachel told me that she will teach me how to make butter if I want.

I shall be very, very, happy here if I know that you and dear Papa are well, safe, and happy. Please write to me all the time, dear Mamma, and don't forget me.

Your loving daughter,
FANNY FRANKLIN

P.S. Aunt Rachel and George are both going to write to you. Anyway, I hope George will. He says he is very busy and that if he doesn't write, I am to send his love in my letter. Mamma, please kiss dear Papa twenty times for me. Tell him he must get well soon so he can come home to his little Fanny.

Fanny's letter shows what a kindhearted, loving, little girl she was. We shall see more of her as our story continues.

Chapter 3

DEVELOPMENTS OF CHARACTER

"Come on, Sam," George yelled. "Hurry up! I want my pony saddled."

"Did you say YOUR pony, Master Franklin?"

"Yes, MY pony," George replied rather arrogantly.

"Oh really? I didn't know the pony belonged to you. I thought it was your uncle's."

"Don't get smart with me," said George, beginning to get angry. "It is none of your business whether the pony is mine or my uncle's. You should just mind your own business. When I say I want the pony saddled, then it is your job to do it."

"Someone else may have a different opinion about that," replied Sam. He was the yard man, gardener, and groom. George's arrogant manner offended him. "I'm not trying to fight with you," he added. "I must say that I have lived at The Elms a long time. I have never been ordered around as much as I have been since you came here three months ago. I don't see any reason for it, either. I don't mean any offense, George, but I am not your servant. Mr. Gray was the one who hired me. He is the one who pays my wage."

15

"Well," George Franklin demanded very angrily, "tell me this. Does he pay you to act smart and not do what you are told?"

Sam did not answer him, instead he returned to the job he had been doing when George so rudely interrupted him. Impatiently, George walked back and forth in the yard for a minute playing with his whip. Suddenly, he walked up to Sam and said in a tight, angry voice, "Are you going to do what I told you to do? Yes or no?"

"Well, Master Franklin, if that's the way it's going to be ..." returned Sam, standing up, looking the boy straight in the face. "If I must choose either yes or no, then I say no. If you will listen to me for a moment," he added respectfully, "I'll tell you why."

"I am not going to listen to you," cried young George Franklin as his pride and arrogance boiled over. "I'm not going to stoop down to your level in order to argue with you. I'm just going to ask my uncle whether trash like you should be allowed to insult me like that!"

Sam interrupted, "You had better stop right there, Master George. We don't let anyone call us bad names in this part of the country. As for asking your uncle about me, you're welcome to do that. Maybe I will have something to ask him, too." When he had finished saying this, Sam returned to his work.

George Franklin walked away with an angry, red face. A few minutes later he found Mr. Gray over on another part of his farm helping some workers.

"Are you very busy, Uncle James?" asked George.

"I'm not too busy to listen to you, my boy. Is there anything 1 can do for you?" asked the farmer kindly.

"Thank you, Uncle. I want to talk to you about Sam Robins. I have something to tell you," George told him loudly, feeling important.

"Really? What is it? Wait a minute, though," added George's uncle. Looking at George's face, he very wisely guessed it was about something which made George angry. "If it is something that is not good, then we had better walk over here a little ways. There isn't any reason for these men to hear what we are talking about," said Mr. Gray in a quiet, low voice.

"I don't mind if anyone else hears what I have to say, Uncle," replied George.

"Maybe I do, my dear boy, so I think my idea is best." Mr. Gray led him away from the others.

"No one can hear us here," he said. "'So now, did you want to tell me something about Sam Robins?"

"Yes, Uncle. He has been very arrogant to me, very arrogant indeed."

"I am very sorry to hear that, and I am also very surprised, too. I always thought Robins was unusually civil and polite. George, please tell me, how was he arrogant toward you?"

"Well, I only wanted him to ..." George then went on to tell his uncle as much as he could remember about the conversation, or rather the argument, he and Sam had. To give him credit, George only told the truth and nothing but the truth. He was taught that dishonesty was disgraceful to a gentleman. Not telling the truth is a disgrace to any other person as well.

George probably did not think about dishonesty being a sin against God, who is Holy and true. The boy would have hated himself if he had purposely hid the truth or exaggerated. In this case, he thought he had such good evidence against poor Sam that he did not need to exaggerate at all. That is why, when he had finished telling his story, his uncle took him by surprise.

Mr. Gray coldly asked, "Is that all, George?"

"Yes, Uncle James, I think that's all," the boy replied, but he was very confused.

"Didn't Robins give you any reason why he refused to saddle Wallace?" Wallace was the pony's name.

"No," said George. Then he added, "I remember now that he did say something near the end about explaining why he would not do it. I did not bother to listen to him because he had been so arrogant to me before."

"Well, right now, let's forget about how arrogant he was. Don't you think, my dear nephew, that it would have been a very good idea to hear his reasons anyway?"

"Yes, Uncle, it would have been if he hadn't been so smart to me at the very beginning," George persisted.

"Well, George. I hope you don't think I am being arrogant towards you, too, but I am going to defend Sam. I'll tell you why he could not obey your orders when you gave them to him."

George turned very red. He didn't say anything. His uncle went on, "There are two reasons why Sam could not help you out right when you asked him to. First, I had put him to work on a job. I told him not to do anything else until he finished that job. The second reason is that when I went into the stable this morning, I noticed that Wallace is starting to get lame. I gave orders not to ride him, so he could rest. I intended to tell you about this and to tell you that you have ridden the pony a little too hard lately. I didn't see you and in the meantime, I came over here to check out a problem my men had. You see," continued Mr. Gray softly, "Robins was just obeying my orders when he disobeyed yours."

"If he had just told me that, then it would have been alright," said George.

"You even said yourself that you would not listen to what he had to say."

"I meant that it would have been better if he had told me that at first. Instead, he argued with me and criticized whatever I said. I was not going to put up with that," George said very angrily.

"Calm down, George. Calm down," Mr. Gray interrupted, "or even I might have to criticize the way you are speaking to me." Then he added, "It would be best if we didn't talk about this any more right now. I am sorry if you are disappointed that you can't have any fun with Wallace today. I am sure you understand why Wallace has to stay in the stable."

It is very possible that George understood this. Unfortunately though, his pride was hurt. He was still very angry with Sam Robins. George felt angry with his uncle, too, although he did not tell him that.

George Franklin's ego had been questioned. George thought that his uncle had not paid enough attention to his complaints. Instead of accepting his uncle's good-natured invitation to walk across the farm with him, he grumpily went back home. As he went by the farmyard and saw the man who made him angry, George angrily shouted and cursed at Sam.

No doubt, Sam Robins would have been wiser to ignore what the boy said. If Sam was going to answer at all, a soft answer that turneth away wrath, would have been better. However, Sam was hot tempered, and he had good reason to be so angry for being attacked with words.

It started a great argument between him and George that is quite unnecessary to repeat here. Mr. Gray, returning home by a different way then usual, interrupted them in the middle of the argument.

"I'm very glad you are here, sir," said Sam as Mr. Gray came up to them. "I want you to tell me, please, who the master is here."

"I'm glad you came too, Uncle James," said George. "I want to know ..."

"Would both of you be kind enough to be quiet right now?" Mr. Gray said sternly. "I have already heard enough. Sam, you can go on with your work. George, please come with me into the house. This is not the right place for you." Saying this, the farmer began to walk away.

"Sir," Sam Robins pleaded.

"Uncle James," George coaxed.

"I will not listen to anything right now," Mr. Gray said quietly. "Sam, you know I always mean what I say. You, George, you must learn that, too. I will talk with both of you some other time, not right now."

George did not argue any more with his uncle's decision. He saw that it would be useless. He went back to the farm house, into his room, and shut the door. Sam went on with his work.

*Have you cooled down enough yet
to hear what I have to say, my dear boy?*

Chapter 4

MORE CHARACTER DEVELOPMENT

"Have you cooled down enough yet to hear what I have to say, my dear boy?" Mr. Gray asked his nephew several hours later when they were together.

"I have been cool enough all day, Uncle," George Franklin replied, trying to sound careless.

"Your body is probably cool enough. You spent several hours in your room without a warm fire on this cold day," George's uncle said sternly. "That's not what I meant, and you know that very well. Can you listen to me now without getting proud or angry?"

"It's not fair to say that I am proud and hot tempered. Anyway, I'm not," George said and flipped his head.

For a second you could almost see a little smile on Mr. Gray's face. A look that was much more serious than before soon replaced it. He did not speak for a little while. Then he said with a sigh, "I haven't accused you of being proud and bad tempered, my dear nephew. Are you sure that you haven't accused yourself? George, remember the warning God's Word gives us. 'If we say that we have no sin, we deceive ourselves, and the truth is not in us.' We all have faults."

"I never said that I don't have any faults," George said quickly.

"I'm glad. There is still a lot of hope for you," Mr. Gray said more cheerfully. "Now getting back to what I wanted to say. I have to tell you that you were very wrong in the way you behaved toward Robins today."

George's cheeks started to turn red. He didn't say a word as his uncle continued.

"I said just now that I never accused you of being proud and hot tempered. I must tell you that the way you acted today showed a very arrogant attitude and a huge lack of self-control. You took advantage of your wealth and being my nephew when you treated Sam that way. You irritated him by giving him harsh, unreasonable commands. Then you insulted him by teasing him about his poverty and lack of education."

"You and Sam have been talking about me. He has made you believe a lot of stories," George exclaimed. His face was still red with anger.

"I've talked to Sam since this morning, George. He spoke about you, among other things," Mr. Gray calmly replied. "Don't you remember speaking to me about Sam this morning?"

An even deeper color of red crept up into the boy's cheeks and forehead. "That ... that was different," he stammered.

"I don't see very much difference, my boy. When he offended you, you complained. Sam felt offended, so he complained. What is the difference, George?"

George Franklin couldn't help seeing that his uncle was right, but it made him even more angry. Again, it showed one of his weak points.

"I'm not a servant like Sam Robins is," he said boldly.

"Because of that, you should be more respectful and considerate of his feelings."

"Feelings! As if those kind of people have feelings," George muttered to himself.

His uncle heard what he said. For a moment, the sadness he felt for his nephew changed to anger. Soon it left, and his sorrow became deeper than before. He saw that he had to deal with much naughtiness and arrogance of heart.

It's not that this was the first time George had shown any bad attitudes. During the three or four months that had gone by since he came to live in his uncle's house, he had shown selfishness. He had acted so arrogantly towards those he considered beneath him that he quickly became very unpopular.

His uncle noticed this. Without being obvious, he kindly and gently tried to keep this evil tendency of George's under control. He thought now would be the right time to teach the stubborn boy a lesson.

"I see," he said after thinking for a moment. "I can see that you do not understand anything about having mutual respect for others. You aren't in the right mood now to benefit from what I have to say. Therefore, I must use my authority. I will ask you first. Are you willing to apologize to Robins for your rude language?"

"Apologize! Apologize to a servant?" exclaimed George. "Especially after everything he said to me?"

"You mean, after everything you provoked him to say. You should think about this, George. It should make you more willing to get matters settled when you consider what really happened. Your mistake caused him to commit his own mistake and act unwisely. Yes, you should apologize. I won't say anything to you about what is expected from a gentleman. I know you think you are one. I must remind you that the Bible tells us to confess our faults to one another. The Lord Jesus Christ also commands us to be willing to forgive and to be forgiven by any brother we have offended."

"I never thought you would take that man's side against me the way you are, Uncle James," the boy cried with injured pride and vanity.

"I am taking your side, my dear boy. I am taking your side against what is unfriendly and wrong," said his uncle kindly.

George Franklin could not see or understand this. He had been used to having strict authority over his father's servants. No one had taken the time or effort to teach him how to deal kindly and fairly with everyone; including servants. George had not learned that brotherly love included all men, women, and children. Now, when he was required to humble himself before what he called a "common farm servant," he saw nothing except cruelty and unfairness.

Mr. Gray was ready for George's angry and proud refusal to humble himself this way. He proceeded to gently but firmly forbid his nephew from talking to Sam Robins anymore. "You will come to me," he said, "when you want something done that he can do for you. I will tell him for you."

"Uncle," George began in astonishment.

"I'm not going to let you argue about it with me, my dear boy," said his uncle. "You might not understand my reasons now if I gave them to you. The only thing I will require of you is obedience. Do you understand?"

Yes, George understood. He rebelled against it. The boy thought he needed someone constantly to help him with his various activities. Sam had very conveniently and usefully filled this need. Now to be immediately cut off from this everyday resource would be a serious loss.

Besides this, he imagined that his uncle's command to him was the same as a great defeat. He had expected a triumphant victory. This hurt his pride terribly. There was nothing to do about it, though. George stomped away angrily, determined to act very dignified and not to ask for anyone's help again.

George acted very independent for the next couple of days. The winter sun shone bright and warm for several days. The snow melted off the roads. It was perfect weather for riding a horse, but George was too stubborn. He wouldn't ask his uncle to have Sam saddle Wallace. He could have saddled Wallace himself, but he couldn't bring himself to admit his defeat.

During the third day and all that night it snowed. When morning came there were deep piles of snow covering the ground. The roads were just right for a sleigh ride. George knew his uncle would let him use one of the sleighs if he asked. George had too much pride to do that. It didn't make any difference to George that his uncle was as kind as ever to him and that he never again mentioned their little misunderstanding.

Fanny could see there was something wrong with her brother. She didn't know what it was. She looked concerned and unhappy about the way her brother was pouting and carrying on.

One day, George came to the breakfast table with a happy face. As soon as the meal was over, he followed his uncle into the hall. He said, "Uncle, can I talk to you before you go outside?"

"Yes, you certainly can, George."

"Uncle, I ..., I think ..., I believe ... I was wrong about Sam Robins."

"I'm glad to hear you say that. Well, what do you think you should do about it?"

"I would like to go talk to him and settle things between us. May I go and talk to him? I didn't want to do it without your permission first," George added.

"I am very, very happy that you finally made this decision. I'm glad that you talked to me about it first. Yes, George. Go and talk to Sam as soon as you can. First, if you don't mind telling me, I would like to know what made you change your mind?"

George seemed a little confused as he tried to explain. "Well, Uncle, you know you said something about it being the proper thing for a gentleman to apologize when ..."

He did not finish his explanation. His uncle saw with regret and sadness that it was just another kind of pride which made him try to patch things up when he had offended someone. Only the love of Jesus Christ can effectively teach the lesson, "Let nothing be done through strife or vain glory, but in lowliness of mind let each esteem others better than themselves," Philippians 2:3.

I am afraid that George Franklin was as proud as ever after he apologized to Sam, and Sam forgave him. George was proud of his humility.

He showed his terrible arrogance with Mr. Paris.

Chapter 5

MORE CHARACTER
IS REVEALED

George Franklin's selfish attitudes showed almost every day in one way or another. For instance, he expected his sister to do exactly as he told her. If he decided to take a walk, he might demand that Fanny go with him. He didn't care if she was busy doing something else or if she didn't want to go.

George's unkind attitude would have caused many fights if Fanny had been as selfish and stubborn as her brother. However, she usually gave in to his demands. She would still have had a great deal of trust and respect for him, if it wasn't for another one of his bad character traits. This one was the cause of many troubles. We shall soon find out what it was.

George also showed his terrible attitude in the arrogant way he acted with Mr. Paris, his tutor. We saw the disrespectful way George wrote about this gentleman before he met his teacher. Unfortunately, this disrespect grew when George found out that his teacher, who had an excellent character and many good abilities, was also very poor.

The foolish boy thought that being poor was a very good reason to despise anyone. George didn't bother to hide his unkind, critical remarks about Mr. Paris when he discovered that he wore an old coat and patched shoes. George also despised that Mr. Paris always walked the whole way to The Elms instead of driving.

George's uncle sharply reproved him for acting this way towards his teacher. Mr. Gray pointed out how selfish, as well as sinful, it was to be proud of one's wealth and lifestyle. He insisted that his nephew act properly from now on. To George's credit, he was not rude to Mr. Paris again.

George didn't use a rude tone of authority again towards Sam after they settled things. George was careful, however, to show in many other ways how much better he thought he was than the poor servant. This is the way George treated Mr. Paris and all the people who worked for his uncle.

We have talked about George Franklin enough for now though. It's time to talk about his sister.

Fanny Franklin was not proud or selfish. She was a very kindhearted and loving little girl. Everyone around her always loved her because she was so honest and unselfish. In spite of this, Fanny had only been at The Elms a few days when the bad part of her character came to the surface. Her mother had unwillingly written about this in her letter.

Fanny was a sensitive, emotional little girl. When she used her emotions properly and kept them under control, then people loved her because she was so free and impulsive. There were many times though, when her emotions got the best of her. She would become very angry and violent and lose control. It is quite true that little Fanny was an emotional girl.

You may think that Fanny didn't have very many reasons to get upset. She had many thoughtful friends who wanted her to be happy. If hot-tempered people waited until they had a good reason to be terribly angry, then they never would be upset. It must be admitted, however, that Fanny was pro-voked.

Although her brother didn't seem to know what his own weaknesses were, he knew what Fanny's were. He loved to tease her about it. "I like to watch Fan throw her little temper tantrums," he would often say when he and Fanny were with other people. Then he would laugh at his poor sister and tease her about how silly she was. Of course, this only made matters worse.

After he had succeeded in making her a little bit angry, he would say. "See, didn't I tell you? Look at how red she is turning. Why, Fan, your cheeks and ears are as red as fire."

Unfortunately, whenever he made this mean remark about her cheeks and especially her ears, she would always get angry and lose her temper. In these rages, Fanny hardly knew what she was saying or doing.

After Fanny's rage was over, she was always terribly sorry that she had lost her temper. She was especially sorry if she had hurt anyone she loved. It's true that the little girl did try to control her quick temper. When she was in a better mood, she seriously promised many times never to lose her temper again if she could help it.

For some reason, when she was tempted to get angry again, she forgot all her good promises. With her own willpower she had built walls to hold in her feelings. These would come crashing down and anger would rush into her soul like a flood of water. Sweet little Fanny was always sinning, repenting, and sinning again. She couldn't seem to stop.

Mrs. Gray lovingly tried to help her niece solve her distressing problem. Eventually Fanny learned to behave properly when she was with her aunt. However, Mrs. Gray knew that she wouldn't always be there to control Fanny's outbursts. It was really up to Fanny to change herself. Sadly enough, Mrs. Gray had been right when she had told her husband that they would have a problem not only on their hands, but on their hearts as well, when they cared for her sister's children.

One day Fanny said, "Aunt Rachel, would you mind ... I mean, can I ask you to do a really big favor for me?"

"Yes, you may Fanny. I don't think there is anything you could ask me to do that I wouldn't gladly do for you. So, what is it?"

"Thank you very much, Aunt Rachel. Well, it's about Susan Watson. I want her to stay overnight a few days and play with me. Is it all right? I mean, could you ask her if she'd like to come, please? I'd really like to have her come to visit."

Now we should explain that one day Mrs. Gray and her niece had gone to Westshire. They spent most the morning there, shopping and doing errands for Mr. Gray. In the afternoon, they visited one of Mrs. Gray's friends, who was taking care of a little orphan girl. The little girl was about Fanny's age. They played together for several hours while the ladies visited.

When it came time for Mrs. Gray and Fanny to leave for home, Fanny could hardly bear to leave her new friend. Fanny liked her a lot. That is why she had built up the courage to ask her aunt if Susan could stay with them for a few days.

Mrs. Gray thought about it for a little while before she answered. Susan Watson was a happy, talkative little girl. Mrs. Gray knew that she was obedient and had very good manners. She also knew that Susan had been carefully raised and taught well. She would probably be a good influence as well as a good friend to her niece. Mrs. Gray also thought that it would be a special treat for Fanny, since she didn't have any other friends at the farm, except her brother, George. She knew that Susan Watson would love to visit them. It might also be very good for her since she was an orphan.

Who isn't interested in orphans? Who isn't glad to show them respect and love? No one, surely, who has a heart to sympathize with human sorrows.

These thoughts went quickly through Mrs. Gray's mind before she answered Fanny's question. Suddenly, another thought came to her which made her hesitate a little bit longer. Maybe her face showed what she was thinking, because Fanny's eyes filled with tears.

She whispered to her aunt. "You don't want to invite Susan, do you? I'm afraid I know why."

"Why, Fanny?"

"You think ... Please, Aunt Rachel. Were you thinking about my temper?"

The poor girl could hardly find the courage to say this. Then she put her little hand on her aunt's arm. Fanny looked up into her face so meekly and beggingly that Mrs. Gray would have had to have a cold heart not to be touched by Fanny's sadness.

"What do you think, my love?" she asked, gently pulling Fanny closer to her and giving her a kiss. "If I am willing to trust you, can you trust yourself to do what's right?"

"Oh, Aunt Rachel, I'm sure I could. I'm almost positive I could," and after saying this, Fanny stopped.

"You're almost sure of what, my dear?"

"That you can trust me. I never, never could be that naughty to fight with such a darling as Susan. She's a poor orphan without any father or mother."

Fanny cried a great deal when she said this, for it touched a very tender place in her heart. It reminded her of her own parents and her father's sickness and her mother's grief. Right then she almost thought that she was being selfish for wanting a good thing that her parents couldn't share. Especially when they might be feeling very worried and sad at that very moment.

After a little while, Fanny calmed down. She was sure that she couldn't possibly lose her temper with such a sweet and lovely person. She made many serious promises to be careful to control her emotions the whole tine Susan was there. Mrs. Gray finally agreed to invite Susan to stay for awhile at The Elms.

"It might be good for Fanny," she thought again. "It might be a good example for her to see how a calm child acts. It would be very pleasant for the girls to share lesson times with a friend. It may also help the poor orphan to be friends with her because Fanny will probably be well known and wealthy when she is older."

Mrs. Gray said, "I will trust you to keep your word, my dear Fanny. If I can persuade my friend to part with Susan for a couple of weeks, then she will be your guest. If she wants to, she can even come home with us today."

It did not take much persuading. Susan was delighted with the idea of spending a long, nice vacation at Mr. Gray's comfortable farm house.

The days went by very happily at The Elms. One week and then two weeks went by, and still the young friends didn't have an argument. They didn't even disagree with each other quietly in their own thoughts. They sat together and did their school work in the morning. In the afternoon, they did their sewing or embroidery. They took walks and played together. There was not even the slightest sign of any dislike towards each other. All this time, Fanny was unusually agreeable with everyone around her. She carefully guarded her temper. Once or twice George had teased her and tried to make her upset. Fanny patiently ignored him. She did begin to say something angry back at him and then stopped herself in the middle of it. Mrs. Gray had seen all this and was very happy about it. She congratulated herself because her experiment was working.

One unhappy afternoon, Mrs. Gray left the two girls alone together for an hour to play. Suddenly, she heard a loud cry come from the room where they were playing. When she quickly went to see what had caused it, she saw little Susan crying. She was covering her stinging, red cheek with her hand. Fanny was pale with anger, standing a little farther away. Her aunt noticed that she already looked very guilty and ashamed of herself.

For a second or two, Mrs. Gray was so surprised and disappointed that she could not talk. Before she had time to ask a single question, Susan ran to her for protection. Trying not to cry very hard, Susan said in a quiet, shaky little voice.

"Please, Ma'am. Will you take me back to Westshire today?"

"Yes; my dear child, you can go back home if that is what you want to do," the farmer's wife said kindly. "First, I would like to know why you want to go home so quickly. What happened to your cheek – the cheek you are trying to hide from me – to make it look so streaked and red."

"Please, Ma'am. I don't really want to tell. Please, don't ask me to tell you," Susan said looking confused. She tried to escape from the lady who had put her arm around her so she wouldn't be afraid of Fanny.

By this time Fanny's short, little tantrum was over. Her heart was full of sadness and guilt. Taking big gulps of air, Fanny rushed forward and threw her arms around her hurt, little friend. Fanny touched Susan's sore cheek.

"Oh, Aunt Rachel, I have been very, very naughty again," she wept. "It was all my fault. How could I ever do that, darling? Susan dear, please forgive me. I didn't mean to do that. Oh, Aunt Rachel. I have been so wicked ... so sinful! Oh dear, what shall I do?" Poor Fanny cried all this and more from her heart as she hugged Susan. She even knelt beside her to beg her forgiveness.

We do not need to say any more about this incident. We don't need to tell the reason the fight began and the quick, angry actions that followed. It is good enough to say that Susan did not hesitate to forgive Fanny.

Still Susan asked again, "If it's all right, Mrs. Gray, I would rather go home to Westshire as soon as possible."

That day Fanny lost her young friend. She cried quietly as she sat alone at her lessons. All her recent comfort and happiness was gone. She humbly accepted her loss. She knew that her kind aunt had good reason to be upset with her.

Even though we have not told everything that happened when Fanny got angry at her guest, Mrs. Gray found out. She knew how innocently and unintentionally the argument began. Even Mr. Gray was very stern and quiet. This was surprising because he had grown very fond of his niece and usually wasn't strict with her. Her brother, who was usually so thoughtless to her, seemed sorry about Fanny's disgrace and what had happened.

Now that Fanny knew she had been wrong, there was something that was even harder for her to take. "The spirit of a man will sustain his infirmity; but a wounded spirit who can bear?" Proverbs 18:14. Fanny's spirit was wounded. In her heart, she knew she was guilty. She knew she had sinned by not treating the people she loved the way she should have. She also knew that she was very guilty in the sight of God, her Heavenly Father.

Quite a few days went by before the humble girl got enough courage to look at her aunt's troubled face. Many more days went by before she could think about her terrible behavior without starting to cry. She promised herself that she was never going to lose her temper again! Being sorry and having good intentions could not undo what she had done.

After quite awhile, Fanny decided she would write a letter to Susan begging her for forgiveness. She wrote Susan a sad little letter which could hardly be read without crying. When Susan Watson read it, it touched her heart. She wrote back such a sweet, loving answer that Fanny was even more sorry that she had ruined their new friendship.

Fanny wanted so much to ask her aunt – and she would have been so humble – to invite Susan to The Elms again. Fanny didn't dare ask.

Chapter 6

THE CLOVER FIELD

One morning, several weeks after Fanny and Susan had their big fight, the family was eating breakfast. One of the field workers came into the room to talk to Mr. Gray about some farm business. The hired man was just about to leave when he suddenly remembered something. He stopped at the door and said, "I almost forgot, sir, but have you looked at the five acre clover field lately?"

"No, Reuben. The last time I saw it, it looked like it was doing well. Why do you ask?"

"It looks good in some places," the man said, "but I went up that way last night. I thought it looked strange in some places out toward the middle of the field. I walked through it and looked. Sure enough, the weed has spread into it really bad."

"The weed, Reuben? What weed?"

"The weed with the ill name, sir. It is such an ugly word that I don't want to even say it. You know. The one ... I mean ... the one that we call by that short name around here. I don't know what its real name is."

"Yes, Reuben, I know which one you mean. Are you sure it's growing in the clover?"

"I'm positive, sir. I even saw it myself. It has grown so much that it has spread over several large areas."

"Then that's the end of one of my clover crops, unless we can kill the enemy," Mr. Gray sighed. "I'm sorry, but I don't know if we could have done anything about it anyway. I'll go and look at it as soon as possible."

"The weed with an ill name? What kind of a weed is that?" George Franklin asked his uncle when the man had left. By now George had started to be a pretty good little farmer. He was always interested and curious about things that had to do with his uncle's land.

"It is a very bad weed, George. It's very destructive and poisonous. It spreads very fast. You can come along with me right now. You can see the harm it has done and what it's doing now."

In less than an hour the farmer and his nephew were ready to walk out to the field. They just stepped out of the hall when Mr. Gray suddenly thought of something. He turned around and said, "Maybe Fanny would like to take a walk with us. It's a beautiful day for running in the meadows. Would you like to come along, Fanny?"

Fanny always loved to go with her uncle as he went around the farm and did his work. In a few minutes she had put on her broad-brimmed hat and was ready to go.

The five acre field was at the other end of Mr. Gray's farm. It lay right next to another farmer's land. Mr. Gray's neighbor could have learned some good things about farming from Mr. Gray if he wanted to improve his farm. He didn't, and so the two farms always looked very different from each other.

On Mr. Gray's side the ditches and hedges were always neat and cared for. They prevented the land from being flooded when the men irrigated. Mr. Gray made sure that fertilizer was put on his crops every year so they would be healthy. The crops that were raised in this clover field were always strong and weed-free, unless something unexpected happened. This was the way Mr. Gray cared for his whole farm.

On the other hand, Mr. Pearson was a careless, lazy farmer. Some of the dams had broken, and they were never fixed. Garbage filled his ditches. This made it very hard to irrigate and drain his fields properly. Many times, pools of swampy, stagnant water covered it. It was never fertilized either. It wasn't able to grow healthy crops. Weeds were a problem because no one took time to get rid of them.

Even during a really good season, Mr. Pearson's crops were worth very little.

We could write a lot more about the differences between Mr. Gray's and Mr. Pearson's farming. It would take us too long. Let's go back to George and Fanny Franklin. They were walking across the meadows and corn fields with their uncle, wondering about the weed with the ill name. Reuben told such a bad story about this.

In less than a half hour Mr. Gray and his young relatives reached the clover field. They could smell its sweet perfume drifting by in the gentle morning breeze.

Well, I don't see anything wrong.

It was a pretty sight. The clover plants, healthy and tall, were blooming with red flowers. They

46

looked beautiful up against the bright, green clover. The delightful, humming music of bees filled the air. Country people who pay attention to these things know how much busy little bees like a clover field covered with flowers.

"There doesn't seem to be anything wrong here, does there, George?" the farmer said after carefully looking across the whole field.

"Well, I don't see anything wrong," George replied. Then he added honestly, "I don't know very much about that kind of thing though."

"What do you think, Fanny?" Mr. Gray continued.

Fanny said she didn't know anything at all about clover and clover fields. She thought the flowers were very pretty and they smelled wonderful.

"Do you see any of the weeds Reuben told you about, Uncle James?"

"Not here, my boy, but I see something suspicious out there in the middle of the field. Let's go in and have a look."

"Won't we hurt the clover if the walk on it?" asked Fanny.

"We might hurt it a little, but we'll have to take that risk. Sometimes its necessary to suffer a little damage in order to do what is good when we are trying to get to the root of evil things. That's the way it is with other things besides farming, too."

"What does he mean?" Fanny thought to herself.

"For instance, there are weeds that grow in the human heart. It's a good idea to reach them and, if possible, get rid of them. Even if it's hard to do. Don't you think so, my dear?" said her uncle.

Fanny said yes, at least she thought so.

"Sometimes when we are doing this, we come close to trampling down some of the finer, better feelings that are growing there. That is where we stern old folks who make ourselves 'teachers of babes' are often wrong, I'm afraid."

"What does Uncle mean?" Fanny wondered again. "It wouldn't surprise me if he is thinking about me and my hot temper."

"I wonder ... is Uncle James thinking about me and my pride?" George whispered to himself.

Mr. Gray went on talking as though he were just thinking out loud. "There is only one perfect Teacher who never makes this mistake. He is the great Teacher who came from God.

"He never tramples down the good to get the bad. 'A bruised reed shall he not break, and the smoking flax shall he not quench,' Isaiah 42:3. I'm sorry, I'm talking to you in parables. I didn't mean to do that. Well anyway, we are here now. Here's the weed. Fanny, even you can see something here that isn't like it should be, can't you?"

While they were talking, Mr. Gray had been carefully walking through the clover. George and Fanny carefully followed him. Suddenly, they all stopped and looked. They had come to a spot in the middle of the field which looked very different from the part of the field they had just walked through. A small circle of clover was short and dried out. The red flowers were wilted, and the leaves and stem looked yellow. Fanny also thought she noticed an awful smell mixed in with the sweet perfume of the clover. There wasn't even one busy bee working in or anywhere near that circle.

That wasn't all. Almost all the clover stems in front of them had thin, tough, mean-looking weeds twisted around them. The weeds had long, tough roots. They were spreading and covering the ground, and now the good plants were being choked to death.

"Is that the weed Reuben meant?" Fanny asked.

"Yes. It deserves to be called 'a weed with an ill name,' doesn't it?"

Fanny agreed. George was curious and he asked what the short name was that Reuben had said sounded so ugly.

Maybe Mr. Gray didn't hear his question, or maybe he didn't want to answer just then. He just said, "I'm afraid we'll have to look around some more." Then he slowly went on, looking around him as he walked.

"Oh dear, I thought so," he said as they found a much bigger area of clover which had turned black and died. The weed, which was now growing very quickly, covered the ground in its place. The weeds here had also put out new shoots in every direction. They were beginning to take root in the soil. They were choking and killing all the clover plants around them.

"See how the damage is spreading here?" Mr. Gray said. "Something must be done soon or else the whole crop will be lost."

"It smells so awful," Fanny said, and it was true. The decaying smell of the dead plants was quite sickening. As for the bees, they had clearly flown far away from that part of the field.

The farmer was still looking at the damage done by "the weed with an ill name." He just pulled up one of the weeds to show his nephew and niece. "See how deeply the roots have grown down into the soil and how many there are."

Just then they heard a voice coming to them from across a nearby hedge.

"So, Mr. Gray, you have some of it too, I see." George knew, it was Mr. Pearson's voice.

"Yes, I've got some of it just like you say," answered the careful farmer.

"See," the careless farmer taunted, "you can't keep the weeds out all the time even with all your weeding and planning."

"Yes, that's very true, my friend. Sometimes weeds will grow in spite of how careful we are," Mr. Gray told him.

He felt like adding, "especially when we have such lazy farmers for neighbors." He didn't say that though. Instead he just asked his neighbor how his crop was doing. Mr. Pearson also had a clover field which was located on the other side of the hedge.

"You should come take a look," Mr. Pearson invited.

So Mr. Gray, George and Fanny went up to the hedge and looked over. One look was enough to convince them that "the weed with an ill name" had found a happy resting spot there, too. It was a sad sight. Half of the clover crop had already died. The weed had taken its place and was clearly spreading very quickly.

"This is really bad," said the wiser farmer. "It looks like the damage has been going on here for quite awhile."

"I'll bet it has," replied the other.

"What are you going to do, Mr. Pearson?"

"What am I going to do? Nothing, of course. What's the use, anyway? It will cost more time, trouble and money to get the weeds out of the ground than the crop it would save is worth. Who knows if I could save the crop anyway?"

"If you had caught it in time, Mr. Pearson ...," Mr. Gray began.

Mr. Pearson interrupted him rather impatiently, "For some reason I knew you would say that. I'm not sure what you say is true. It isn't quite that easy to get rid of the problem."

"Well, we'll have to see, my friend. There's one thing I am sure of. Looking at it and talking about it will not do any good. It's time for me to get back to work, so I must say goodbye."

Mr. Pearson said a friendly goodbye, too. Then Mr. Gray walked home with his nephew and niece.

Chapter 7

ANOTHER VISIT TO THE CLOVER FIELD

That same morning Mr. Gray called several of his hired men from the work they were doing. He gave them pitch forks and shovels. He took them all out to the clover field. For several days they worked hard. They did more on this part of the farm than on all the rest of the farmland put together. When the workers finally finished, Mr. Gray invited George and Fanny to come out and see the clover field again.

It took a little while for them to walk out there. On the way they walked through the healthy part of the crop. They came to the part of the field which had been overrun and ruined by the destructive weed. They understood even better than they had before how much damage, loss, and work that "the weed with an ill name" had caused.

There were wide spaces in the field that were completely bare. In the bare spaces, the workers had plowed under the soil so it looked like it usually did after harvest time in the fall. It was clear to see that every corner of the field had been carefully searched. In every place where they found a weed, it was carefully dug up. There were several piles of

The men were tossing the weed piles into the fire to be burned...

dead, stringy, poisonous weeds mixed with the dead clover. In one large bare spot, someone had built a fire. The men were tossing the weed piles into the fire to be burned so they couldn't take root again.

While they were watching, Mr. Gray picked up one of the weeds. He called his nephew and niece over to look at the strange weed and see why it was so dangerous. First, he showed them the roots. He told them that they spread out in all directions underneath the ground. Long before a farmer knew they were growing in his field, the weeds had begun to steal the minerals and water that the good crop needed.

Then he showed them the long, twisted and almost leafless stems of the bad plant. He explained how they tightly grabbed hold of the first tender plant they came near and wrapped themselves around it. Then they would immediately throw out a couple of small suckers, poking them into the tender plant and sucking out all its juices until it had died. That is how the weeds grew and spread.

"Do you think you got rid of all the weeds now, Uncle James?" Fanny asked. She, as well as her brother, thought their uncle's description was very interesting.

"I doubt it," he replied. "If I'm very careful to keep an eye on them, most of my poor clover crop will be safe."

"How did 'the weed with an ill name' start growing here, Uncle James, and what's its real name?" George wished to know.

"I will answer your last question first," Mr. Gray said. "In this part of the country, the weed is usually called 'hell-weed.' It's an ugly name, just like Reuben said when he told me he had discovered it here. It's probably called that because of its terribly destructive qualities. It means that it is something to guard against and avoid. The scientific name of the weed is 'cuscuta.' When we get home I will show you a description of it in one of my farming books."

Mr. Gray continued, "How did it get here? Well, its seeds were somehow carried here. They began to grow just like other ordinary plants usually do. I don't like to accuse any of my neighbors, but I'm afraid there's no doubt where the seeds came from. Let's go and look at Mr. Pearson's clover field."

One glance told them there wasn't any hope left of saving Mr. Pearson's crop. He hadn't even tried to stop the weed from spreading, so it had quickly taken over the whole field.

"What are you thinking about, George?" Mr. Gray asked suddenly, as they were on their way home again.

"I think it's awful!" George exclaimed.

"You said that before," Mr. Gray said with a smile, "but what is awful?"

"That Mr. Pearson, or anyone, should be allowed to do such damage to other people as well as to themselves by being lazy and careless," said the boy.

"You are taking it for granted that the seeds of the 'weed with are ill name,' as we will keep calling it, blew across from his clover field into mine?"

"Yes, Uncle James. Don't you think they did?"

"You think that the weeds matured and went to seed because of his poor farming?"

"Yes," George said again. "Don't you think that's why it happened?"

"Well, I must admit that you are probably right. It's true that Mr. Pearson's style of farming does give me some trouble sometimes. For instance, I remember a few years ago when a few thistle plants came up in one of Mr. Pearson's corn fields. Instead of chopping them down, which would only have taken a few minutes, he ignored them. He let them grow among his corn until they flowered and went to seed. Then one windy morning when I was walking across my farm, I saw the air filled with clouds of thistle down. I knew that every piece of floating fluff had a seed in it. This was the first time I knew anything about my neighbor's thistle crop. Then it was too late to fix the problem."

"What happened?" asked the children.

"Well, the next spring both my neighbor and I had very healthy crops of thistles. I spent a lot of extra work and money that whole year and two or three years after that trying to get rid of them. Mr. Pearson deserves some credit though. For once, he began to work hard to get rid of the weed from his own land. Since then, we haven't had any more thistles."

"You must have been so mad. I mean, I would have been so mad," Fanny cried. "I would have had a big fit if I had seen that nasty thistle down flying all around like that."

"You probably would have, my dear," Mr. Gray said quietly. "I'm glad it was my land and not yours that had the problem. Now, do you both want me to tell you something that I've been thinking about?"

"Yes, do. What is it?" they asked curiously.

"I've been thinking how we often let valuable lessons go by without learning from them. I remember an old saying about this. 'While the faults of our neighbors with freedom we blame ..."

"We tax not ourselves though we practice the same.' Right?" George exclaimed. "Uncle James, even you don't always follow your own advice!"

"You're right. I know that I don't follow it as much as I wish I did. Anyway, what we saw today and what we have been talking about just proves those very important, serious truths which we find so easy to forget. That is that 'one sinner destroyeth much good,' Ecclesiastes 9:18, and that 'none of us liveth to himself,' Romans 14: 7."

Mr. Gray continued, "In the small affairs of this life, we often see how one man's carelessness about his own everyday business can hurt many others. We see this problem in our tempers and habits. No one can give in to sinful attitudes. Those are the weeds that grow in the human heart, causing pain and suffering for everyone around them. That is how it is with spiritual matters, too. The man who despises God hates his own soul. He scatters his seeds of sin in the souls of others. Unless divine mercy intervenes, there will be a large crop of sinfulness and wretchedness."

Mr. Gray finished talking. Since his young friends did not say anything more, they all walked quietly the rest of the way home.

Chapter 8

THE LECTURE

During the long winter evenings and the shorter spring evenings it was a habit for Mr. and Mrs. Gray and their nephew and niece to sit beside a cheerful fire. They would spend the evening talking with each other or reading. Often Mr. Gray or George would choose an interesting book and read out loud to the rest of the family. Mrs. Gray and Fanny sewed or knitted quietly. In a few months it would get too hot to sit by the fireside, but summer wasn't here yet. They could enjoy these happy little get-togethers for a while longer.

The night after they visited the clover field for the second time, Mr. Gray took a heavy book down from his bookshelves. He found the article he mentioned earlier in the day. He read Fanny and George a long, interesting description about "the weed with an ill name." It told about the plant's appearance, natural history, habits, and the most effective methods of preventing its damages. When Mr. Gray finished reading the article, he closed the book. He sat there for quite awhile without saying anything. He looked as if he was thinking very hard about something.

Mrs. Gray looked up from her work and said rather teasingly, "A penny for your thoughts, James?"

"You can have them without paying for them, Rachel," her husband replied, pulling himself away from his distracting thoughts.

"Let me guess them, okay?" said Fanny. "You were thinking about Mr. Pearson and your poor clover field, weren't you?"

"Well, you're partly right, but you're not quite right, Fanny. Yes, I was thinking about my clover field at first. Then I began thinking about other kinds of fields and other people's fields as well as my own. For instance, I was thinking about your field, Fanny, and also about yours, George."

"Uncle James, we don't own any clover fields, or any other kind of field either," Fanny said with a little laugh.

"Are you sure?"

"Well, unless you mean – maybe I know what you mean," the little girl said. Then she hesitated for a minute.

Mr. Gray smiled and encouraged her to go on. "Well, what do I mean?" he asked.

"That our hearts are our fields." After Fanny said this, she leaned down so closely over her embroidery that it looked like she was counting her stitches. When he heard what Fanny said, George began to look a little uncomfortable himself. He liked his uncle very much. However, he didn't always like it when his uncle talked about serious things, especially when they were personal and to the point.

George sighed and thought to himself. "Oh, great. Now we are going to get a lecture."

George was right when he guessed that his uncle was going to talk seriously about their faults. In fact, during the whole time Mr. Gray had been busy with the weedy clover field, he had also been thinking about how he could use the situation to teach George and Fanny some important lessons. This is why he had invited them to go with him to the field the first time. It was also why he took them to look at it after the workers weeded it. He had been sitting quietly because he was thinking about what to say to them.

George thought that a lecture was always a harsh accusation. He was wrong when he imagined that his uncle was going to give them "a lecture." This was not the way Mr. Gray liked to deal with anyone. He mixed kindness with disapproval, and he tried to follow the dear Savior's example.

"Never trample down what is good in order to get at the root of what is bad," said Mr. Gray. We could write more about his very good attitude, but instead we will let the kind uncle speak for himself.

"You were right when you guessed what I was thinking, Fanny," he said, smiling thoughtfully. "Yes, in some way our hearts are our fields."

"I suppose you think some of us have very poor soil, don't you?" George asked him.

"Oh, Yes. Very poor soil, my dear boy. I know that I have good reason to think and say this about everyone's hearts. Scripture is definitely a more qualified authority than I am. God's Word says, 'The heart is deceitful above all things, and desperately wicked; who can know it?' Jeremiah 17:9. 'Out of the heart proceed evil thoughts, murders, thefts, false-witness, blasphemies,' Matthew 15:19. I think you and I are right, George. If our hearts are compared to fields, then our soil is definitely very, very poor."

"What's even worse," Mrs. Gray added, "is that the soil isn't only poor, it's dirty and full of bad, harmful seeds as well."

"That's right," her husband agreed. "It's just the same as all the other land I have ever planted and brought to a harvest. Weeds seem to grow very easily, and they always spring up by themselves. The ground is naturally full of these kinds of seeds, or at least it seems to be. If you leave it alone, before long you will have many kinds of useless, harmful plants growing. You don't have to plant them or look after them at all. It's only the good seed that has to be put into the ground and cared for when it starts to grow."

George shrugged his shoulders. "I wonder what Uncle James is trying to get at now? That was stupid of me to interrupt him," he thought. Meanwhile, his sister had stopped counting stitches and was now timidly watching her uncle's face. She was thinking to herself that she knew a little bit about some of the weeds that grew in the human heart.

"Uncle James, your land must be pretty free of weed seeds and everything by now, isn't it?" George asked after a second or two of silence. He was hoping to change the topic of conversation by using a little bit of flattery.

Mr. Gray shook his head and smiled. "You're giving me too much credit, George. I'm not such a good a farmer that I've been able to get rid of all the weeds by now. No, that hasn't happened yet. Weeds will grow, my boy, and plants follow the law of nature. There is a proverb that says, 'Ill weeds grow well.' If the seeds aren't already in the ground, then they get carried to it through the air. If they are buried so deep that they can't begin to grow, then they will lie there safely, who knows how long, until the soil is turned over. Then up they spring and begin to grow and thrive."

"Are our hearts like that?" Fanny asked in a soft, small voice.

"Yes, dear, I'm afraid they are," Mr. Gray answered. "No one can tell how many evil seeds are buried and hidden in our hearts just waiting for a good time to spring up. The Lord Jesus Christ knew this very well. That's why He taught His disciples to pray, 'And lead us not into temptation, but deliver us from evil.' That prayer has a lot of meaning."

Mr. Gray went on, "The fields in our hearts are full of bad weeds either in seed or in growth. By this, I don't mean that they are never able to grow good, useful crops. A Divine Power has planted valuable seeds in the fields of every one of us. The Bible says, 'Every good gift and every perfect gift is from above, and cometh down from the Father of lights,' James 1:17. George and Fanny, don't you think that if we have good seeds planted in the soil of our hearts, then it's worth it to take care of them and make sure they grow?"

George couldn't deny this. It made good sense.

Fanny said, "Oh, yes! I'm sure it is a good idea to take care of them."

Gradually and purposely, Mr. Gray turned the conversation. It became more serious. He told them about God's Holy Word and its instructions. It warns us and calls us to be "the good seed of God's kingdom." He told them that God had put the generous and loving emotions in our hearts. It is the Holy Spirit's gracious influence that is necessary for the seeds of the heart to live and grow strong, just as the air and warmth are necessary for the seeds of the earth.

Mr. Gray said that education helps feed the heavenly plants so they grow in the human heart. Every person must be very careful or these plants might be destroyed. He then reminded his nephew and niece of Solomon's counsel, 'Keep thy heart with all diligence; for out of it are the issues of life,' Proverbs 4:23.

Mr. Gray continued, "Do you remember one of the parables Jesus told about a nobleman who was traveling to a far country? Before he started on his journey, he called his servants together. He gave them some talents to use while he was away. (Matthew 25:14-30, Luke 19:12-27) God prepares the fields of our hearts. He plants good seed in them, but he leaves it up to us to take care of this good seed when it springs up. We must keep out the weeds that might choke the tender plants and kill them."

Then the wise farmer explained the different kinds of weeds that grew in the heart. The ones that caused so much unhappiness and required so much watching and hard work.

When their uncle mentioned these, George's face clouded over. Fanny's eyes filled with tears. She put her head down to hide her red face. Both of them expected to hear their uncle say something about the seeds in their own hearts.

They were right, but Mr. Gray was very gentle and loving. He told them about the sinful desires that are in the hearts of children. He quoted the verse of a hymn.

Soon as we draw our infant breath,
The seeds of sin grow up for death;
Thy law demands a perfect heart,
But we're defiled in every part.

"Usually," Mr. Gray explained, "these seeds of sin are indigenous. Maybe that's the way they always are, though. Fanny, do you know what the word indigenous means?"

Fanny said that she didn't know. Her brother did. "Indigenous means anything that is natural to an area of the country or in the soil," George proudly explained.

"That's right, George," his uncle agreed. "I'm afraid that the seeds of sin, and the 'plants' they grow, are almost always natural to the poor soil of our hearts. Sometimes these seeds come from outside influences. They are brought into our lives and dropped there. It's just like my clover field. There still may be seeds of 'the weed with an ill name,' deep down under the ground in my field, even though the weeds grew from seeds that came from my neighbor's field.

"It's the same with people. 'Evil communications corrupt good manners.' Young people especially are always being exposed to bad examples and worldly ideas. Then impure, sinful thoughts quickly take root in their hearts and cause a lot of damage there."

"Well then, Uncle James." George said, "if people put such sinful things into other people's hearts and minds, how can they help it? If people's hearts are full of bad seeds, then how can they stop them from coming up?" George asked these questions rather triumphantly. He was afraid that his uncle was thinking about some bad weeds that were in his heart. George figured he had found an argument that would be hard for Mr. Gray to answer.

"I'll say something about that later on, George. First, I'm going to say a few things about the damage I was talking about." Mr. Gray reminded his nephew and niece of how "the weed with an ill name" had destroyed part of his field. It destroyed even more of Mr. Pearson's clover field. It had quickly killed all the good crop around and made the ground bare and empty.

"So," he continued, "we can't let one single 'weed with a bad name' have its own way in our hearts. It will choke and destroy everything that is praiseworthy and good. It will make our hearts empty and bare. Then all the good seeds of education and knowledge, all of our kind and gentle feelings run the risk of being even worse than wasted.

"Now, George," he continued. "I will answer your question. Do you remember the two clover fields? One of them, and I don't have to say which one, will lose its crop. All the plants that looked so promising just a few weeks ago, have withered and died. They can only be used for fuel. The good, or at least what used to be the good, and the bad will all have to be burned together.

"In the other field," Mr. Gray went on, "the seeds started growing just like they did in the first field. If the weeds had been left alone, the same thing would have happened. You know they were not left alone. As soon as we discovered them, we did what we had to do in order to get rid of them. I won't tell you all the hard work it took for us to do that. I hope my hired men and I have been success-ful and saved the main crop. I am sure we'll lose some of it, but at least we won't lose the whole crop.

"That's kind of the way it is with the fields of our hearts, George and Fanny. Evil seeds and weeds with an ill name as well as an ill nature appear and grow there. What if we left them alone, Fanny? Should we do that?"

Fanny had been listening carefully to every single thing her Uncle said. She had completely forgotten about her embroidery, which she had put down on the table. It was easy to see that she was very interested in hearing what her uncle had to say.

Once or twice her face had turned red. It wasn't because she felt angry. Instead, it was because she understood what he meant about the wicked weeds that were in our hearts. It's no wonder that she felt confused and embarrassed when Mr. Gray suddenly asked her the question. However, this didn't stop her from answering very seriously in a quiet, worried voice. "No, we definitely should not!"

"Would you want to have them chopped down and pulled up, my dear?" her uncle asked. "Would you want your poor heart to be plowed under and hurt in order to get rid of them? It is very rough and hard, just like it was in my clover field."

"I know, but I think it would be the best thing to do. In fact, I know for sure that it would be the best thing to do." Fanny said. She was still very serious.

"If you have any interest in your heart, you won't allow these 'weeds with an ill name' to keep growing there. Let me call them by their crude name for once. Don't let these 'hell-weeds' happen to spring up until everything good is destroyed. Then the whole crop is like it has been 'twice dead, plucked up by the roots,' and only fit for the 'everlasting burnings.' Would you chose to let this happen to your heart?" Mr. Gray asked this question with great sincerity.

"Oh, no!" Fanny cried. She tightly held her hands together as she said, "Oh no! Anything is better than that!"

"You are so right," her aunt echoed softy. "Anything is better than that, little Fanny."

George was a little moved, too. His uncle's serious voice and manner had impressed him. Yet, a part of him wanted to ignore this feeling.

"Uncle James," George began. "It's easy to see right away where real weeds in real fields are growing. Then you can begin working on them like you did. How do people find out about the weeds that are in their own hearts? How are they supposed to get rid of them?"

"Those are very important questions," said Mr. Gray. "I will try to answer them. First, let me say that it isn't always easy to find real weeds in real fields. Many times they grow without us ever seeing them. Some of them look so much like good, useful plants that we let them grow together until harvest time. Maybe you think it's easy to get rid of them right away, but wouldn't it be easier just to leave them alone?"

"I guess so, but then you would lose some of the crop," said George.

Mr. Gray answered, "That's true. You sounded just like a wise, careful farmer when you said that. Yes, you would lose some. It's very smart of you to compare that with the time and trouble I have had with my poor clover field.

"Now I will answer your questions. One way to find out about the weeds in our hearts is to watch and examine ourselves carefully. Another way is by comparing what starts to grow there with God's Holy Word. Remember, the Bible says, 'Wherewithal shall a young man cleanse his way? [or in other words, how should a young man keep the weeds out of his heart?] by taking heed thereto according to thy word,' Psalm 19:9. We must compare ourselves and our actions, thoughts, feelings, and desires with what we find written in God's Word. We must also seek the Holy Spirit to teach us. That's the only way we can ever discover all the new weeds and hidden sin in our hearts.

"Another question you asked was about how we are supposed to get rid of them. The only way to get rid of them is always to be careful to watch out for them. We must have self-denial and self-control. We must honestly pray to God to help us in every time of need. Pray as David did, 'Create in me a clean heart, O God; and renew a right spirit within me,' Psalm 51:10. We must try to follow the example of Jesus Christ. 1 Peter 2:21-22 says, 'For even hereunto were ye called: because Christ also suffered for us leaving us an example, that ye should follow his steps: Who did no sin, neither was guile found in his mouth.' We must look to Him as our Savior. He came into the world to 'save his people from their sins.' Matthew 1:21."

After a short pause, Mr. Gray continued, "It might seem hard to be so careful and to have so much self-denial. Of course, it would be a lot easier to leave these 'weeds with an ill name' alone. It would be easier not to worry about them, wouldn't it, George?"

George agreed.

Mr. Gray said, "You always should remember the loss that's involved. There is a loss of the whole crop and all that which is good. God created man for His glory. Now think how sin has brought an everlasting contempt. This is why the loving, merciful Savior says in Matthew 5:29-30, 'And if thy right eye offend thee, pluck it out, and cast it from thee. ... And if thy right hand offend thee, cut it off, and cast it from thee: for it is profitable for thee that one of thy members should perish, and not that thy whole body should be cast into hell.'"

Mr. Gray decided he had said enough for now. He hoped he had started his nephew and niece thinking in a good direction. It did look as though the things he said had impressed both of them. It's true that he hadn't said a word about hot tempers or pride. He didn't even need to mention that these were some of the weeds of the human heart. The children already knew they were.

Chapter 9

THE CONFESSION

The whole time George and Fanny Franklin stayed at The Elms, they eagerly looked forward to getting their mail each week. Their parents wrote them many letters, and George and Fanny never forgot to write back. At first the news from their parents was not very encouraging. The change of climate and surroundings hadn't seemed to help Mr. Franklin very much.

Recently, happier news had arrived. Their sick father was getting stronger and healthier. The dangerous disease he had was going away. Mrs. Franklin hoped and prayed that they would only have to spend one more winter in that warmer climate before she and her husband could return home. When they finally could come home, it would be a much happier time than it had been when they began their travels.

Their mother's good news excited Fanny and George. It helped them look forward to the happy meeting they would soon have. This was better than worrying about how many months they still had to stay at their uncle's farm.

In the meantime, they were busy learning many useful things. They had a lot of free time and they

He was always willing to do errands and ride his horse...

didn't waste it. George really enjoyed helping others in different ways. He was always willing to do errands and ride his horse to Westshire or anywhere his uncle sent him. Fanny had a lot of fun learning how to make butter and cook chicken. She learned many other things, too.

Even though they loved helping around the farm, their aunt and uncle never allowed them to forget their school work. Mr. Paris still taught George his lessons. George deserves some credit. After his uncle scolded him, George acted much nicer towards the gentleman. Fanny carefully learned her lessons each day with Mrs. Gray's help.

It was haying time now. For several days both George and Fanny went out to the hay fields and helped their uncle. With their wooden rakes, they helped gather the hay as best as they could. The purpose of our story, though, isn't to describe what a farmer does. We aren't trying to show how fun and interesting it is to visit a farm house. We have other matters before us.

One evening Mrs. Gray wondered where Fanny was. After a little while, she found Fanny in her own little room crying very hard. The little girl didn't cry very often. Her aunt wondered what could be the matter.

"Are you sick, my love?" her aunt gently asked her.

"No."

"Has something upset you?"

"No, not really," Fanny said. She tried to calm down and look more cheerful. She couldn't.

"I'm afraid maybe you just got too tired," her aunt said. "You worked very hard in the hay field this afternoon."

"Oh, aunt Rachel, that isn't why." Fanny cried. "I feel so sad." She began to weeping again.

Mrs. Gray sat down beside her niece. She held her little hand. "Can I say or do anything to take away your sadness?" she asked.

"I wish you could. Oh, wouldn't it be nice if you could, Aunt Rachel." Fanny cried. Fanny was thinking, "It's no use. No one can ever cheer me up."

"Maybe if you tell me what is wrong, I can help you, my dear," Mrs. Gray offered.

"It's about the weeds," Fanny whispered after a minute or two.

"The weeds?" Fanny's aunt questioned. She hadn't really forgotten. She just didn't think of the clover field and "the weed with an ill name" at that moment. She didn't think of the conversation they had about them during a family evening together. It had been almost a month ago.

"The weeds in my heart." Fanny said in a trembling voice. She leaned her head on her aunt's bosom and added, "I never knew until a little while ago. I didn't know until now what a wicked, wicked heart I have."

Mrs. Gray immediately understood what Fanny meant by "the weeds." She saw what the girl's trouble was. "Are you really sure that now you know what a wicked heart you have?" she asked kindly.

The little girl thought about this. She only knew there was a lot of sin in her heart. "I'm very sure!" she said.

"What made you think about this now, my dear?"

Fanny said that what her uncle said about the bad weeds of the heart had almost scared her at first. This made her think about what would happen to her in the end if she let them grow strong and rank.

"This didn't scare me that much," she went on very quietly. "I thought it was only necessary to watch and be careful. I thought I could keep these weeds from growing."

"Then you forgot all about it, didn't you, my dear?" Mrs. Gray asked after Fanny stopped talking.

"No, Aunt Rachel. I didn't really forget. In fact, I've thought about it a lot since then. That night I made up my mind because I knew what a naughty, hot temper I have. I made up my mind that I would never be so quick to lose my temper again. When George or anybody ... I mean, whenever I've been criticized or teased, I have tried to be good and patient. I have tried so hard." When Fanny came to this part of her confession, she cried very hard.

"Did you find that you weren't good or patient? Is this what you discovered?"

"Oh, Aunt Rachel, it was my heart! I mean my thoughts and feelings," cried Fanny. She was more discouraged than ever. "I can stop myself from talking. Many times I have walked away so I wouldn't lose my temper, but it's still in me just like it has always been. I have had such wicked, dreadful thoughts." The poor girl cried and cried with frustration.

Then she told her kind, caring aunt how she was tempted and tested terribly that very day. She had gone away by herself because she didn't want to show her anger. She became more and more angry when she was all done, and no one could see her. She had wished many evil things would happen to the person who had upset her. After she calmed down, she was shocked with herself. Poor child. It was easy to see that it had been very hard for her. She was very sorry about it now.

"Then you don't think your heart is any more weed free than it was a month ago, Fanny?" Mrs. Gray asked. Her heart went out to Fanny. She was so sad and distressed.

Is this where you've been reading, my love?

"Oh, Aunt Rachel, I never knew before how bad my heart is. It isn't just my temper. There are many other things, too. So many ... Uncle James was sure right when he said a lot of bad weeds grow there. I feel like I'll never be able to get rid of them, never. They will grow stronger and stronger. Then it will be just like Uncle said."

Poor discouraged Fanny! She couldn't go on. She began to cry, because she was heart broken. Her aunt felt sorry for her. She was glad too, but it was not because the little girl was sorry and upset. She hoped and believed her sorrow would turn into joy.

"Fanny, do you remember ..." she started to say. Then Mrs. Gray noticed something on the little dressing table she hadn't seen before. "Oh, I see you have your Bible out. May I look at it?"

"Of course," Fanny said.

"Is this where you've been reading, my love?" asked the kind aunt.

Fanny laid her trembling fingers on a passage the Bible was opened to. "Whosoever hateth his brother is a murderer: and ye know that no murderer hath eternal life abiding in him," 1 John 3:15.

"Do you think that awful warning means you, too?" Mrs. Gray asked after she read it.

"I'm afraid it does, Aunt. If you only knew what wicked thoughts and feelings I had today when George ..." It was useless for her to try. She could not go on.

"You don't need to tell me, my dear child. I don't want to know. There is One who does know, and that is enough."

Fanny said sadly. "I know that God knows." Then she shuddered as though she were afraid.

Mrs. Gray said, "I mean God, our heavenly Father and Friend, Fanny. This powerful and Holy

Being who knows and sees everything we think, say and do. He has given us the beautiful, loving words which come right before the verse that troubled you so much. Do you remember them?"

"I don't remember what came before that. Those terrible words upset me so much, I can't remember any more."

"Let me read them to you. Listen to what our loving Father in Heaven says to us in His Word." Mrs. Gray turned back one page of the Bible and read, "'If we say that we have no sin, we deceive ourselves, and the truth is not in us. If we confess our sins, he is faithful and just to forgive us our sins, and to cleanse us from all unrighteousness.' 1 John 1:8-9."

After reading this encouraging passage, Mrs. Gray reminded the sad girl that God, who is Holy and just, has said that He is "faithful and just to forgive sin." God is able to forgive sin because of the life and death of His dear Son, Jesus Christ. Jesus Christ came into the world to save the sinners, not the righteous. He carried their sins in His own body when He died on the cross. He rose again from the dead and went up to heaven.

He is forever seated at the right hand of God. He is pleading for sinners who know they need mercy and forgiveness and who are willing to put their trust in Him. Fanny listened to all this. Her aunt went on talking about God's promises to every person who truly repents and believes the blessed gospel of His dear Son. Fanny began to calm down.

She said in a quiet, soft voice, "It's very beautiful, Aunt Rachel. It's very, very beautiful."

Don't think that this was the first time the sad little girl had ever heard these wonderful, happy truths found in the Bible. No, Fanny had heard them many times before. She had thought about them many times, too. This time, however, they touched her soul like never before. She had never before felt such a strong, burning desire to have her sins forgiven by the Redeemer. She wanted her heart and soul sanctified and made holy by the Holy Spirit.

She thought it was very beautiful that God loved His people so much. He sent His dear Son into the world to carry their heavy burden of sin. The love of Christ saves sinners. He gave himself as "an offering and a sacrifice to God." Ephesians 5:2.

Then she had another disturbing thought. "If everything I've ever done were forgiven ... all my hurtful attitudes and everything ... oh, dear! Those seeds of sin that Uncle James talked about would grow up again and again every day. That's what always happens to me. When I feel so sorry for what I've said and done and have made up my mind not to do it anymore, it's never done any good. Sometimes I have been just as bad again the very next day."

"It will always be that way, my dear," replied her kind advisor, "when we try to make ourselves holy. When we try with our own strength to pull up those bad weeds in our hearts which bring us so much trouble and loss, then we always fail."

"What should I do then? What can I do?"

"Darling, there is only one thing you can do. Remember who said 'Come unto me, all ye that labour and are heavy laden, and I will give you rest. Take my yoke upon you, and learn from me; for I am meek and lowly in heart: and ye shall find rest unto your souls,' in Matthew 11:28-29."

"Yes," Fanny said, "I remember; Jesus said that."

There was something that stopped her from being encouraged by the gentle invitation. It was this: she knew how sinful her heart was. She knew how easy it was for her to lose her temper. She knew that no matter how hard she tried, she still wasn't able to get rid of this "weed with an ill name." If all this was true, then how could she find peace for her soul?

Even worse, she had found out that this wasn't the only bad weed that was growing in her heart. She was getting very worried. The more she searched that poor soil, the more she was finding all kinds of "weeds with an ill name." They were ready to spring up and choke out all the good seed which God planted there.

How could she have peace and rest, unless it was the kind of rest that was lazy and careless? Her uncle's neighbor was this way with his land. She didn't even want to think about having that kind of a lazy rest. This would only end in everlasting loss.

"Fanny," her aunt said, "when the Lord Jesus Christ was on earth, He said that He did not come to call the righteous, but sinners to repentance. It is the sick, not the healthy, who need a physician, Luke 5:31-32. Does that make you feel a little better?"

"Yes, it does a little. It must be so nice to know and feel it, but ..."

"You cannot make yourself holy. Is that what is bothering you?"

"Yes, Aunt Rachel. I feel like I am worse than ever. I'm getting worse and worse all the time. I can't seem to get away from my naughtiness."

Mrs. Gray turned the pages in Fanny's Bible looking for a certain passage. Then she showed it to her. She said, "Can you stop crying long enough to read this, my love?"

Through her tears Fanny read these words. "Who is a God like unto thee, that pardoneth iniquity, and passeth by the transgression of the remnant of his heritage? He retaineth not his anger forever, because he delighteth in mercy. He will turn again, he will have compassion upon us ... he will subdue our iniquities," Micah 7:18-19.

"Oh, Aunt Rachel!" Fanny cried happily as she saw these last words. "That's what I want. Now I understand. I can't, but God can. I can't, but God will."

"Yes, dear Fanny, by His Holy Spirit He can and will subdue our iniquities. He will destroy the weeds in our hearts if we ask for his blessed help and mean it. He tells us to ask for His help. Luke 11:13 says, 'If ye then, being evil, know how to give good gifts unto your children: how much more shall your heavenly Father give the Holy Spirit to them that ask him?' Fanny, our heavenly Father has many good gifts for those who truly love Him."

Many times, when Fanny went for a walk,
the pretty dove went with her.

Chapter 10

THE RINGDOVE

It was prophesied that the Lord Jesus Christ would "feed his flock like a shepherd," and would "gather the lambs with his arm, and carry them in his bosom," Isaiah 40:11. This was how "the good Shepherd" lovingly treated Fanny Franklin. It was not long before she found peace for her soul by looking unto the character of the Lord Jesus Christ. She asked the Lord to give her that blessed Spirit of Christ and spare her from losing her temper so easily. Her hot, angry temper did not suddenly go away. But the Lord gave her strength so she was not tempted any more than she was able to handle. 1 Corinthians 10: 13.

In fact, Fanny honestly and eagerly prayed the prayer which the Holy Spirit gave us. She asked, "Create in me a clean heart, O God, and renew a right spirit within me." Her prayer was answered. The seeds of sin in her heart lost most of their power. Instead, the seeds of holiness, purity, faith, and love were planted there and began to grow.

Here's one example out of many that shows that Fanny was able to keep the ill weed out of her heart. This was the same ill weed which had given her so much trouble in the past.

Early in the spring, the little girl was given a pretty, white ringdove. Fanny loved the bird very much and she made it her pet. Soon the dove became so tame that it flew to her when she called. The bird would perch on her finger while she fed it from her hand.

Many times, when Fanny went for a walk, the pretty dove went with her. Sometimes it sat on its young owner's wrist or shoulder as she walked. Sometimes it flew around and around in circles above her head. The bird never flew very far away though.

It was the beginning of the second harvest time since Fanny and George had been at The Elms. Fanny was busy in the house when her brother came and told her to take a long walk with him. He said that he had the whole day off to do what he wanted. He knew where they could find a lot of walnuts, and he wanted to go pick them.

If Fanny had done what she wanted to, she would have stayed at home. However, she had become used to George's thoughtless demands. She got ready for the walk without arguing.

They walked through several meadows when suddenly they heard a whirring sound in the air above their heads. In a minute or two Fanny's pretty ringdove flew down and sat on her shoulder.

"That bird is such a nuisance," George complained.

"Poor little Floss," Fanny said to her dove. "Why are you here? You should have stayed at home today."

Floss had not stayed at home. There wasn't anything else to do except take the poor bird along with her. Fanny wished Floss hadn't come. Sometimes her brother got irritated about how much she loved the pretty dove. One day he had even said, "I think you love Floss more than you love me."

She had answered, "Well, Floss never tries to make me mad like you do." That had hurt George's feelings very badly. It injured his pride and ego and perhaps his conscience too. After that thoughtless comment by his sister, he didn't like Fanny's pet very much.

Now Fanny was careful not to pet Floss too much, so her brother wouldn't feel offended and hurt. Feeling neglected, the bird left Fanny's shoulder and flew a little ways up into the air. Floss began flying in wide circles around her head.

In order to reach the woods where the nuts were, they had to leave their uncle's land. They walked through some fields that belonged to Mr. Pearson. One of these was a field of ripe peas, cut down and ready to harvest. They had got to the middle of the field, when suddenly they heard a gunshot nearby. At the same moment poor Floss fell fluttering through the air and landed at Fanny's feet. Floss was still living, but she was wounded terribly. She was dying.

With a cry of agony, Fanny picked the bleeding bird up from the ground and held it gently against her chest. All her care, love, and sadness did no good. Once or twice the poor bird gasped and flapped its wings weakly. Then its eyes grew dull and it laid perfectly still in the child's arms. She still held it lovingly against her chest. Floss was dead.

"Put me down! Let me go! I'll tell my father if you hurt me. The stupid thing was stealing father's peas. I had a right to shoot it. It served the bird right for stealing."

This loud outburst roused Fanny from her sad daze. When she looked in the direction of the cry, she saw that her brother had dashed away from her side. He had caught a boy who was smaller, younger, and weaker than he was. George now held him in his grasp. Fanny knew the boy was one of farmer Pearson's sons. He was a mischievous boy.

It was plain to see that George was very angry. He didn't care whether the bird was alive or dead. He cared about his sister. It irritated his pride and ego that somebody had dared to hurt anything that belonged to him or someone close to him.

George was just getting ready to hit the scared little hunter when his sister ran forward and stopped him. She begged and pleaded with him to stop and leave the Pearson boy alone. Reluctantly, George was persuaded to forget his revenge and let the boy go.

Their little trip to the nut wood was over. With her brother by her side, Fanny tearfully returned home. She was petting her poor dead ringdove the whole way.

"Why didn't you let me punish Tom Pearson like he deserved, Fanny?" George asked as they went along.

"It wouldn't have done any good, George. It wouldn't have brought sweet, little Floss back to life again."

"I know that as well as you do. It would have served Tom right and taught him a good lesson."

"I didn't want him to get hurt," Fanny said.

"You have become pretty merciful," her brother said. "I'm wondering about something, Fanny. Why you didn't lose your temper over it?"

"I wonder why, too," Fanny replied softly, "I'm glad I didn't."

"I don't know why you're so glad. I sure have seen you fly into a big rage over less important things than that."

"I know," Fanny said honestly, "but ..."

"But what, Fanny?"

Fanny didn't answer, and she didn't talk about the subject anymore.

Maybe she thought it was too hard to explain. Maybe she was afraid that her brother wouldn't understand her. Would he be sympathetic when she tried to explain the struggles her soul went through? Would George understand if she told him that she had finally found the strength to control her angry ways? She asked for the Holy Spirit's help often each day.

"Fanny, I can't figure out what has come over you lately," George said in amazement.

"What do you mean, George?"

"I mean you're different somehow. You're less ... I don't really know how to say it. You're less ... No, you're more, more lovable," George said laughing a little. "There, I said it. It's the truth," he added. "I don't mean that you weren't lovable before, that is, when your temper wasn't showing. Now don't start getting red cheeks and ears, Fanny," George said, trying to cause trouble, "because you have a temper of your own, you know."

Fanny knew it was true. For a minute she felt offended by this remark, even though her brother might have meant it as a compliment. The next minute the angry feeling in her heart left. She spoke so kindly to her brother that he felt sorry for what he had said.

"I'll never try to tease you again, Fan" he promised. "Besides, it doesn't work anymore, so it's no fun. It's cowardly of me, anyway."

George was quite right. Fanny Franklin had become lovable. As the ill weeds of the heart are cut down and destroyed, the good seeds of the kingdom of God begin to grow. They bring forth the fruits of the Spirit. "The fruit of the Spirit is love, joy, peace, longsuffering, gentleness, goodness, faith, meekness, temperance," Galatians 5:22-23. There's a poem which says,

The Weed With An Ill Name

When piety in youthful mind,
Like tender buds, begins to shoot,
God guards the plant from threatening winds,
And ripens blossoms into fruit.

Maybe it was only a little thing for Fanny to speak kindly to her brother or to anyone else when she became upset with them. She was patient when she usually would have been impatient. Maybe it was a little thing for her to forgive someone with all her heart, like she forgave the boy who carelessly hurt her by killing her little bird.

When His youngest disciples, as well as his oldest, do these little things, they honor the Lord Jesus Christ. When men see these good works of Christians, they are led to glorify their Father in heaven.

Chapter 11

GOOD SEED SPRINGS UP

A few days after Fanny's ringdove died, a letter from Fanny's mother arrived at The Elms. The good news in the letter made Fanny forget all about her sadness. Her mother had written to say that her father was completely well. They planned to come back to their home in London as soon as possible.

George and Fanny were so excited! That meant that they would be home soon. They started packing their things and getting ready to leave. They had loved staying at The Elms with their aunt and uncle. They really didn't want to leave them. They also had missed being at home in London with their parents. Their aunt and uncle understood how they felt. They were very happy for them.

The parents sent their children several more letters. Then they wrote to say that they had a certain day set for them to ride the train home.

There was one place, though, where Fanny really wanted to go before she said goodbye to her uncle and aunt. For a long time she had wanted to see Susan Watson again. Now she wanted to see her more then ever before. She knew that soon she would be home, and they would live far away from each other. Fanny had often thought about their fight. She recently realized how awful she had been to Susan. This was the reason Fanny wanted so badly to tell Susan how terribly sorry she was. She wanted to find out if Susan really had forgiven her.

Mrs. Gray must have guessed what was going through her niece's mind. She said to Fanny one day, "I'm going to drive to Westshire this afternoon. Is there someone there you would like to see before you leave for London?"

So they both went to Westshire. If it were necessary, we would tell what happened between Fanny and Susan when they met. If Fanny had doubts about her young friend's forgiving nature, they had disappeared by the time they had to tell each other goodbye.

Now we must join George as he prepares to leave. There was something on his mind, too.

"Uncle James, before I leave I would like to tell you something." George stammered awkwardly. He began to look embarrassed. It was the last night the children would stay at The Elms. George was taking one last walk over the farm with his uncle. They reached the five-acre clover field. It had been cut once and it was now almost ready to harvest again. The "weed with an ill name" had disappeared, and so had the bare places the weed had caused. The farmer had worked very hard in the field and had made sure that new seeds were planted in the bare spots.

"Go on, my boy," Mr. Gray said kindly.

"Uncle James, I'm afraid ..., I mean, I want to thank you for being so nice to me since I've been here."

"You're welcome George, even though I didn't do very much. I'm glad I could help you, though you know that," Mr. Gray sincerely told him.

"Yes, Uncle. I know, and I'm glad."

"I certainly enjoyed being with you. I'm glad to see that you did, too. So what are you afraid of then?"

"Well, I'm afraid I've caused a lot of trouble for you sometimes." George had to force himself to say this.

"No, I don't think so. At least, not a lot of trouble, George. What makes you think that?"

"I don't know really, but ... but I was afraid that I had been."

His uncle asked with a friendly smile, "What put such a strange thought into your head, George?"

"I don't know. I've thought that for quite awhile. It was this clover field that reminded me," George answered.

"How and why did it do that?" Mr. Gray asked curiously.

His nephew explained. The field had made him remember "the weed with an ill name." This made him start thinking about his uncle's serious talk about the weeds of the heart. After this, he had started thinking about himself. His conscience had reminded him of many times when the weeds in his own heart had caused a lot of trouble and worry for everyone around him. Now that he was leaving his uncle's house, George was feeling very sentimental. He remembered how his uncle had been so unselfish and kind. George was quite outgoing and usually considerate and caring, so it was natural for him to tell his uncle how he felt.

"You think some weeds with an ill name and nature are growing in your heart?" Mr. Grey asked, after listening to George's honest confession. He was glad that George had been thinking about this.

"I'm afraid there isn't any doubt about it, Uncle James."

"Well, George, what are you going to do about them?"

"I suppose I will have to treat them just like you treated your weeds here. Pull them up and send them to the garbage pile." George was serious and meant it. He said it in a joking way though.

"Well, for instance, which weed are you going to start with?" asked his uncle.

"Which one? Well, I guess pride because I know I'm proud."

"Arrogant, selfish, conceited, and stubborn. Do you include all of these things when you mean pride?" Mr. Gray asked him.

George turned red and hesitated a little. "I never thought of all those things. I suppose they include pride. If pride has to go, all the rest will too, I guess."

"I suppose so," his uncle coolly agreed. "I only mentioned them to show you what a many-headed monster you will have to fight. Let's not change the subject. Well, so you're going to get rid of pride? When do you plan to start?"

George seemed a bit confused by this question. "I ..., I ... hoped ..., I thought I'd already started," he stammered.

"You have? Well, I hope you have success with your job. When you're finished with that weed, what comes next?"

"Do you mean what other weed comes next?"

"Yes. Which one will be next?"

George was very confused. The way his uncle was acting puzzled him. It felt like his uncle was making fun of him. He couldn't figure out how to answer the question either. He had thought that when pride was gone, the field of his heart would be almost totally free of weeds. He thought for a minute or two. Then he said in a shocked voice, "It doesn't seem like you believe me, Uncle!"

"Yes, I do. I believe you honestly plan to conquer the wrong things you see in your character. I think you have miscalculated how much power you have to do this. You'll find that the work is too hard and never ends. It won't do any good anyway."

George looked up in amazement at his uncle's face. It was not like this kind, gentle uncle to sound so discouraging and cruel.

"There's only one way we can get to the root of the sinfulness that is in us," Mr. Gray continued.

"Make the tree good, and the fruit will also be good. Kill the seeds, and the weeds will stop growing."

"I'm afraid I can't do that, Uncle."

"You're right. You can't do it – by yourself. There is One who can. Go to God for help, through the Lord Jesus Christ. Say to Him, 'Take away all my wickedness. Cleanse me and wash my sin completely away.' He will help you to overcome just like Christ also overcame. He will give you victory over the evil tendencies in your heart. You will be 'more than a conqueror through him who loved you.' Jesus is your Savior and example."

This was one of the last conversations George had with his uncle until many years later. The next morning, after a short night's rest, everyone was busy doing last minute packing. George and Fanny were extremely excited. They also felt a little bit sad when it came time for the ride to Westshire. The same horse and the same strong buggy that they rode in almost two years ago took them there.

They bought tickets at the train station for Mrs. Gray, George and Fanny. Then they began their fast ride on the train to London. When they arrived at London's train station, they were overjoyed to see their parents again. They had been apart a long time. We won't tell very much about this happy reunion. There are only a few pages left in our story. We have some other important things left to tell.

After staying in London for a few months with their parents, George and Fanny left home to go to boarding school.

Fanny met many people in this new place. They had all sorts of different tempers and personalities. Fanny Franklin found that it took constant watchfulness and prayer to keep down the bad weed in her heart. She often felt frustrated and angry with her friends. Sometimes quick, hurtful words came to her lips, but the brave young disciple did not stop being careful. She always wanted to learn more about the Savior, Who is "meek and lowly in heart." Every day she asked for "grace to help in time of need." She grew to be a good example of patience and humility to the other children.

Her natural tendencies didn't completely change or reverse, but they were easier to control. Her quickness of apprehension, eagerness, and excitability indeed remained as part of her character. They were no longer employed in conjuring up fanciful insults and injuries, or in resenting real ones.

On the contrary, her nature was kept under control and used in a spirit of universal love to all around her. Her natural characteristics increased her charms and gave additional value to her friendship.

When she left school for the summer, Fanny was well-liked by both her teachers and schoolmates. She went through life making valuable friends because of her great love for others and her life of unselfishness. It had been a blessing that "the weed with an ill name," which in her younger days had threatened to poison and choke out the good seed planted in her heart, had been conquered and pulled up. The beautiful plants that God had planted – long suffering, meekness, and patience – had grown up and taken their place.

Out of all of Miss Franklin's friends, she valued Susan Watson the most. Quite a few years after their first unhappy parting at The Elms, they met each other again. It wasn't long before their feelings toward each other had turned into mutual admiration and friendship. The two young ladies helped each other in different ways. They often met together to study the Bible and encourage one another in their Christian walk through life.

Now what do we have to say about George Franklin? We will end our story just like we began it, with a letter from George. Here it is.

Dear Uncle James,

Ten years ago you and I took a walk together to one of your clover fields. You have probably forgotten all about it by now. I haven't. You probably don't remember either, why we were looking at the field.

I remember that you had trouble with that field during the summer. You had to work hard to get rid of "the weed with an ill name" that had started growing in it.

That evening after our walk, you told me some very important truths. You told me about the bad

Dear Uncle...

weeds that grow in every human heart. You thought they were so important that you told me again.

I remember that I wasn't very glad you did it. I thought you were being too hard on me. Now I can see that you were very nice when you talked to me. I didn't care then. I didn't believe what you told me, because I just didn't want to. I didn't listen to you at all. For some reason, I knew that you were probably right. I promised that I would get to work and get rid of "the weed with an ill name." I knew a lot of it was growing pretty tall in my heart.

Do you remember what I'm talking about now? Do you remember how you told me that I could never do it on my own?

That's what I didn't believe. You showed me some of my sinful, dangerous attitudes. I couldn't pretend they weren't there. I was pretty sure that I'd be able to get rid of them. I was determined to do it, too.

Uncle James, I hardly knew how evil my own heart was. The Bible tells us that he that trusteth in his own heart is a fool. I was that kind of a fool.

Soon I got tired of working so hard on it. What was the use of trying to get rid of my bad weed? As soon as I thought I had cut it down, it popped up again and grew taller than ever. In fact, it grew so tall that I soon earned a bad reputation around school. My schoolmates and friends only knew me for the very thing I thought I was conquering. This made me decide to quit my useless struggles. I was disgusted. I said to myself, "if the 'weed with an ill name' wants to grow, then let it."

I grew older and was around more people. I found out that it was very inconvenient to have the bad reputation that I had deserved to earn. I began to hide my bad attitudes. I let pride, arrogance, selfishness, and conceit stay in my heart. On the outside I put on a mask of friendliness and generosity, and sometimes I even added humility.

I don't know if I really deceived anyone else. I know for sure that I didn't deceive myself. The weeds didn't worry me much, anyway. I didn't care whether I killed them or not. All I wanted to do was cut off some of the leaves.

No, I never tricked myself. I didn't know that at the time. Now I can see that while I was trying to trick others into thinking that I was something I really wasn't, other bad weeds were growing steadily in my heart. These weeds were starting to show in the way I lived and acted every day.

After quite awhile, my eyes were opened a little. I saw that my heart was in a terrible condition. It made me stand still and pay attention. My letter would be too long if I told you exactly how this happened. I will only say that seeing only a little part of the evil that I had in my heart terrified me.

I couldn't help but think then about Mr. Pearson's clover field. Do you remember how the whole crop was ruined after he let the weed run riot in it? It was destroyed and had to be burned. I thought about how you had compared his field to people whose hearts have become full of sin and wrong attitudes.

I knew that I could not let it go on anymore. If I didn't quickly get rid of these bad weeds for good, then much worse things would happen. I knew I would have eternal loss and misery in the end. Once more I decided to try very, very hard to get rid of these weeds. I can't tell you how miserable I was or everything I did to make myself better.

Sometimes I thought I had finally done it. Then I was quite happy and proud. Then something else happened that showed me how completely wrong I was. This made me realize that the weeds I thought I had killed were actually growing faster than ever.

I was still trying to make myself holy. I was even hoping I would eventually succeed when I read one of Jesus' parables.

I found it in Matthew 12:44-45. It was about the unclean spirit that went out of a man. The spirit had walked through dry places trying to find a place to stay. It hadn't found any. Then the unclean spirit said, "I will return into my house from whence I came out." Then he returned to the empty house with seven other spirits. They were more wicked than he was. They all lived there. The last state of that man was worse than it had been at first.

This made my soul tremble, Uncle James. I couldn't help thinking that the same thing would happen to me as it had to that man. What if I did succeed in getting rid of my sinful attitudes and habits for a while? What if I threw them out of my heart? Who could tell if they would come back and be seven times stronger than they had been before?

Then I remembered what you said to me the last night we were together. You spoke with love and kindness, but you gave me a strong warning. "Make the tree good, and the fruit will be good. Kill the seeds, and the weeds will stop growing." I told you that I couldn't do it. You said that you knew that, but God could do it for me only if I went to Him and honestly prayed for His Holy Spirit to help me. He would give me the strength to overcome just like Christ also overcame. I'm not sure these are the exact words you said ten years ago, but I remember that this is what you meant.

Uncle James, I'd never thought about this very much before. I'd never thought it would be worth it to go to God for help. I think it was because I was too proud to do it. Now I've started to truly believe that I could do nothing without His help.

I went to the Lord and prayed these verses from the Bible. "Lord, save me, or I will perish." "Jesus, thou son of David, have mercy on me." "Create in me a clean heart, O God; and renew a right spirit within me. Wash me from mine iniquity, and cleanse me from my sin."

Then I began to see something I had never seen before. I knew now that the only way the love of sin, that "weed with an ill name," can be destroyed in a person's heart is if the Holy Spirit shines God's love and forgiveness in there. We need faith in the Lord

Jesus Christ and we need to ask Him for His Spirit. He will give it.

Uncle James, I hope you don't think I'm boasting. I sure don't have any reason to boast. I don't even dare think that the bad weeds in my heart are all dead yet. I hope they are stunted and weaker. I am so glad that God says in His Holy Bible that He which hath begun a good work in us will perform it until the day of Jesus Christ, Philippians 1:6.

Your loving nephew,
GEORGE FRANKLIN